PART 1

FROM TITO TO DROGBA

Production : 7 ÉTOILES Éditions

First draft of artwork : Hippolyte Kouamé

Layout and artwork : 100%FREE

English Translation : Yeri de Londres

Editorial co-ordination :
DAGAN EDITION and BOOKS OF AFRICA LTD

Communication

Guillaume Bertel - COMQUEST

DIDIER DROGBA

PART 1

FROM TITO TO DROGBA

Based on a indea by

GABIN BAO

TEXT AND DIALOGUE

GABIN BAO

ILLUSTRATION

PIERRE SAUVALLE

COLOURING

PICTOON STUDIOS

étoiles
EDITION

BOA
BOOKS OF AFRICA.COM

Legal deposit January 2014

First edition

ISBN : 978-2919613076 - DAGAN Jeunesse, Achères, France
ISBN: 978-0-9926863-7-6 - BOOKS OF AFRICA LTD - London, United Kingdom

For the first edition published in Côte d'Ivoire
Copyright 7 ETOILES Editions - Gabin Bao

For the French edition
Copyright DAGAN Jeunesse

For the English edition
Copyright DAGAN Jeunesse

A CIP catalogue record for this book is available from the British Library.

FROM 1978 TO 1983

1978, Yopougon Andokoi: a neighbourhood where kids start playing football very young. I grew up in this part of Abidjan. I couldn't escape my destiny.....

ALLOCO ALLOCÒ... HOT ALLOCO !!

HA HA HA

PASS...PASS THE BALL HERE...

Nice hot fried plantains !!

On the final days of her pregnancy, my mum was surrounded by her family and friends who were there to support her.

"Be strong, it will be ok, you'll have a beautiful baby. Take my word for it.

A few days later ....

Oh thank you! God has heard you."

Welcome my baby!

"He is really a fine baby; he's going to be a famous man one day. That's my prophecy for you, my dear".

May god protect him"!

5

To the great surprise of the whole family, I started walking when I was only 6 months old.

Look, he is walking already".

Quite normal darling; he is as strong as I am!

HA HA HA HA

HI HI HI HI

AREUAREUU

"My grandson will be stronger than a lion".

GAGAGGAA

HA HA HA HA

« Look Auntie, he can walk very well! Have you given him a nickname?"

"TITO! like the leader of Yugoslavia"

My father took me outside to take my first steps with the local kids.

HAHAHA

"Uncle"! "Uncle" " What's his name?"

"His name is DROGBA DIDIER TEBILY but you can call him Tito.

Then all the children started clapping their hands in rhythm to make me walk.

TITO TITO TITO... TITO...

CLAP CLAP CLAP

6

A few months later at the age of 5, my destiny took a turn...

The drone of the diesel engine of a taxi interrupted our game.
We wondered who was going to get out of the taxi.

It was my uncle, Michel Goba,
my father's younger brother.

Uncle Michel has arrived!...
Uncle Michel has arrived!

"But who do I see?
Is this my boy
Tito?!"

Yes it's really
me!

Ha ha ha, my little
Tito you have grown,
haven't you?

Yes I have - and
I play football
like you, uncle.

Wooooow!
An Argentina team
jersey!

French money –
it's beautiful.
I am going to keep it
as my treasure, uncle.

When I go back I would like to take Tito with me, to live with us in France.

Is that for real uncle? So I will see lots of white people then!

Hahaha, yes Tito my boy, you will see lots of whites over there!

Would you like to go with Uncle Michel then?

Yes mum, I'd like to go to France!

Alright then, it's OK if you want to go with your uncle. No problem

My parents were happy about this but....

....I'd have to leave my mother, and that made me sad.

9

The day had come for me to travel to Paris. I had tears in my eyes as I got in the car which was taking me away from my parents.

Sniff, sniff...

Hey young man, you will see. You will like Paris.

Come on Tito! You're a big boy now!

Sniff, sniff...

Mum, I don't want to go to France any more. I want to stay with you and my friends!

You need to go to France to study. And then, you will come and see us during the holidays.

Bye Tito, goodbye...

Tito, don't forget us!

Bye Tito!

My son, when you are in France, make sure you work hard at school and be respectful towards your seniors, your uncle, your aunt and your friends. You will have to be a role model for your friends.

OK dad!

Attention please, the flight to Paris is now boarding at Gate 3.

When I arrived in France I stayed with my uncle and his wife.

Tito, we are going out after lunch to buy you some new clothes... Would you like to come along?

Yes, Uncle Michel.

We can also get you some chocolate if you like?

When I come back from training, I will bring you a nice football.

Thanks uncle, thanks auntie!

Each time we went out I gazed at the beautiful buildings... and all these white people around me...

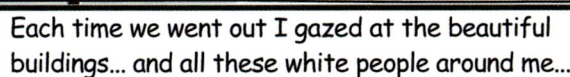

Uncle, everything looks so clean here!

You can say so. Hahahaha!

I think that's the example we should follow in Africa instead of going into wars all the time.

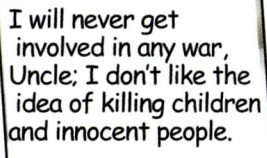

I will never get involved in any war, Uncle; I don't like the idea of killing children and innocent people.

You are right, Tito.

What's this street called, Uncle?

My uncle and his wife did their best to make me happy and provide me the best education.

On my first day at school in France, my uncle and my aunt came with me to make me feel at ease and encourage me.

Good morning, we have brought our little Didier along!

Oh little Didier is cute!

Thank you Miss!

Tito, you've not forgotten to put a bottle of water in your bag?

No Auntie I haven't!

Sitting in class, I realised that I was the only black. That intrigued me...

At lunch time my uncle would come and pick me up from school. That was when he would give me some advice about school life and life in general.

Well, did you have a nice day?

Yes Uncle.

Very good! It's important to work hard, to be a role model by your behaviour, Tito. You must never cheat in class.

Uncle, me I don't like cheating!

That's very good Tito. You can come along with me to the training this afternoon if you want to!

Oh yes Uncle, but will I be allowed to play too?

Yes of course but you will have to play off the pitch.

That's great, Uncle, thanks!

Arriving in Abidjan, my mother came with one of my aunties to pick me up at the airport.

Tito Tito!

Mamaaaann !!

Tito Tito!

You've grown tall and handsome. I love you, my Tito.

Hahaha.... hahaha

Welcome back my son. Dad is waiting for you at home.

It's good to see you mum.

While I was away my parents had moved to Yamoussoukro

14

GOOOOOOOOALLLL
HAHAHHA HAHAHA
HAHAHHA HAHAHA
1-0!
TITO TITO...
TITO TITO...
We'll beat you! We'll beat you!
Our captain comes from France! He's really strong!
We don't care! We'll Gboro him and we'll win!
HAHAHA HAHAHA

Back from my stay in Ivory Coast, my uncle came to pick me up at the airport.

Did you have a good trip?

Yes Uncle !

I hope everything went well, big boy...

Yes very well Uncle. I have made myself some new friends.

Let's go home and eat - then later on we can go to the training.

Cool!

You are back at last. I've made you your favourite cake.

Tito, can you fetch me a nappy so I can change your little cousin.

Auntie, can I change him please?

Of course, sweetheart. Go on.

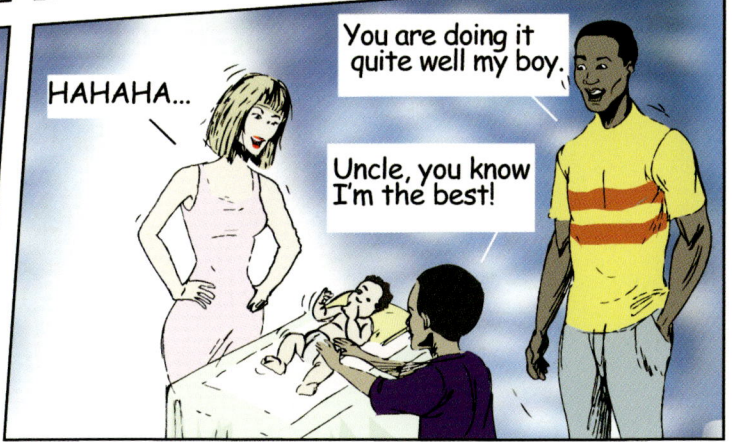

HAHAHA...

You are doing it quite well my boy.

Uncle, you know I'm the best!

Because of my passion for football, my uncle, who was a role model for me, decided to register me at Dunkirk football club and they helped me get my first licence as a football player! I was only nine years old!

One training day, my uncle Michel Goba came to see the coach to find out how my game was progressing.

Time was going by and I realized that I was big for my age. I let my hair grow into a short afro. At that period I was something of a loner.

Watch the game carefully. When I grow up I will also play for Marseille.

OK that's good Tito.

DRRRINNNN

DRINNNNG

Hello

Good morning, may I speak to Michel please?

He's not here.

May I speak to Tito if he's around?

Hello Mum it's me!!

My son! I did not recognize your voice, you talk like a man on the phone.

Come on Marseille. Come on OM!

Come on Marseille. Come on OM!

As soon as I put the phone down I went back to watch the game, Marseille had just scored.

Ha ha ha! Mum, how are you? I miss you so much! When are you going to come and see me?

Very soon! What about you? How are you keeping? Are you doing well at school?

Yes mum, I am.

I will call you again next week. Take care, my son!

In 1990, my uncle told me that my dad was soon coming to live in France because of the crisis in Ivory Coast. I was thrilled at the thought of seeing my dad again, and seeing the rest of my family a little later.

My father had come to visit us at his brother's house. I was happy to see him back with us in France, but soon he would see my school reports.

Good morning dad!

Good morning uncle!

HA HA HA

Good morning children, I am so happy to see you.

Michel is not in yet?

He has gone out but I think he won't be long now.

Ok, what are the news here?

Our little Tito is going to have to repeat year 9.

Oh really?

So Tito, you are not working hard enough then? You spend all your time thinking about football.

I think that you will come and live with me for a while because your uncle and aunt are spoiling you too much and you are becoming a big baby again.

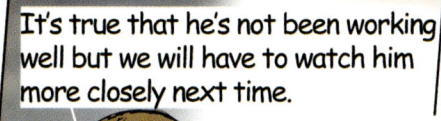

It's true that he's not been working well but we will have to watch him more closely next time.

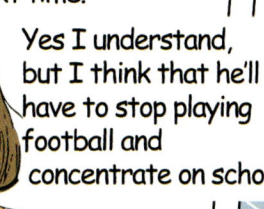

Yes I understand, but I think that he'll have to stop playing football and concentrate on school.

We'll still see you every weekend, shan't we Tito?

Do you really think that's the right thing to do?

Yes I think it's the best. Anyway I'm coming back in three days to pick him up. He will stay with us for a while.

From that day on I went to live with my parents. But the hardest thing was having to stop playing football.

I went to stay with my parents and there were 8 of us living in a small apartment in Levallois.

Children what do you want to do when you grow up?

Daddy, I'd like to be a teacher.

What would you teach? And why?

A lecturer in French at university teaching young people to have a good knowledge of French.

Well done son! What about you Tito?

Dad, I want to be a doctor to heal the children all over the world when they get ill - and especially you and mum.

Ah very good! But in order to reach your goals, you have to work hard at school, Tito.

So you will go and live with your cousin at Poitiers so that he can help you with your _____ studies.

No problem dad, I will do my best to work hard this time.

From 1993 to 1995
When my dad came from work, he gathered the whole family around to share some good news.
Children! In a couple of days we shall move out because I have finally found...
a bigger apartment... in Antony.
Ha that's good news daddy!
GREAAAAAT!
OK but I won't be able to see my girlfriends any more.
Don't worry darling - you will make some new girlfriends.
Well if you don't want to move you'll have to live here all by yourself ... Hahaha
A few days later, we had started moving our stuff out.
There's no more space. Put it down at the side.
Hey Tito, Tito! You're moving?
Hello Mark, we're moving to Antony. But don't worry I'll come and see you often.
We'll miss you in our team, Tito.

Months went by and I had started training again with the Levallois club. At the age of 15, I could not wait to live my passion - football! I was using all kinds of tricks with the help of my mother and sisters to go for training so that my father would not send me on one of his errands.

Mum, where are you? We need to talk.

Mum!

I'm in the kitchen, I'm coming.

Mum I am planning to go for training in a few minutes.

OK no problem. What else do you want to ask me?

Oh mum, dad is in the living room, you see... and I don't want him to know that I am going for training.

Ok I understand, if he asks you any questions, tell him that you are going to do your homework at your friend's place.

Thank you mum, that's why I love you so much.

Big sister, I am off to football. Mum knows about it but tell dad that I am going to a friend's house to prepare a class presentation...OK?

OK brother you can trust me!

So I was a secret player, creeping off to training sessions with a wink from my mother.

All the best Tito, work hard and don't come back too late.

OK! Yes, sure! See you in a bit!

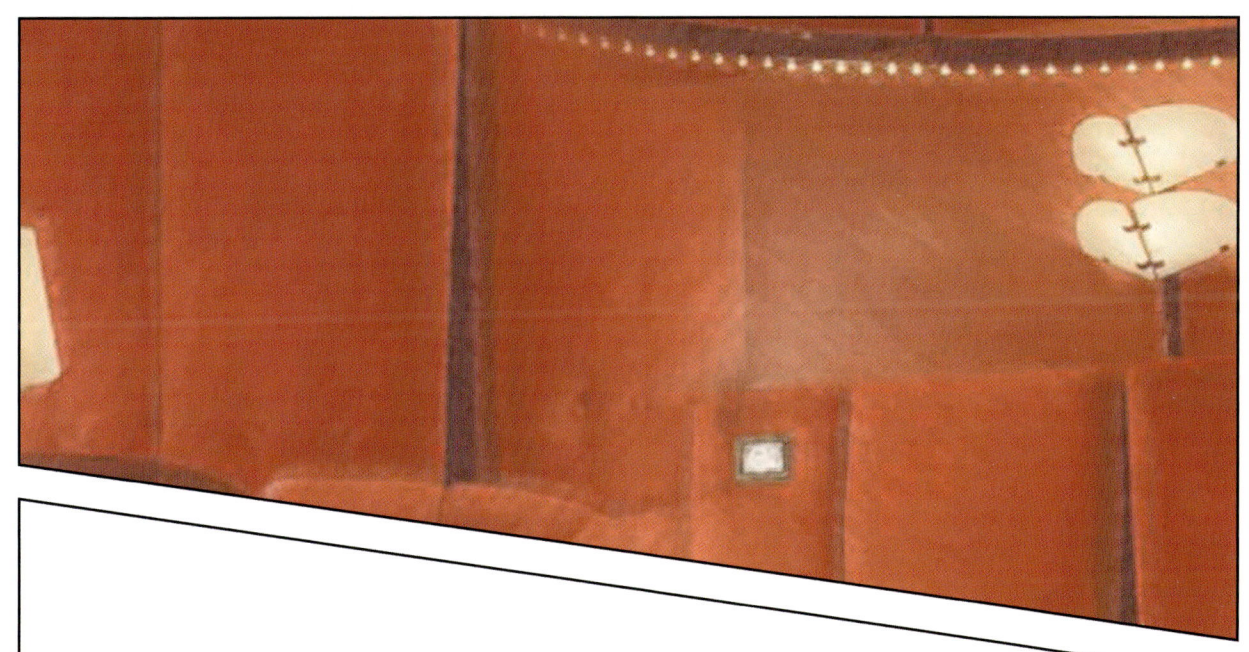

Meeting Lalla turned me into a little romantic lover; not only was I spending all my time writing love letters which I would spray with perfume before posting them, but also I was her most constant visitor.

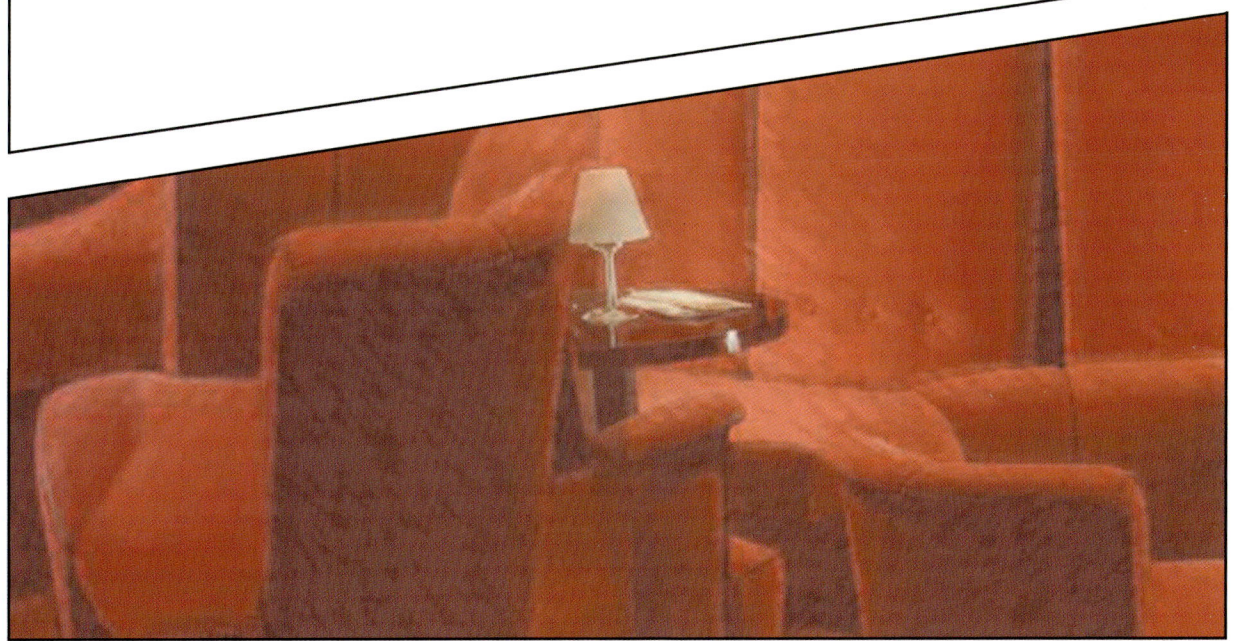

My uncle really wanted to see me succeed in football; he was moving heaven and earth to make me get there.....

Hello Tito, I have got you enrolled for a trial at Rennes football club. I have got some good contacts there so you're going on my recommendation.

That's great!

I can't wait to go.

The trial will be in 3 days so get ready so you can perform.

Thank you for coming Mr Drogba. Your uncle Michel Goba told me you were coming. Get changed quickly then come and show me your prowess, big boy.

The day of the trial I bumped into one of my team mates from Levallois who had also come to try his luck. We were 23 players being trialled and that showed how hard the selection was going to be.

During the trial I did my best.

As my dad would always say, every effort deserves a reward.. and I was one of only two players selected to continue the trial.

Back at Levallois I felt bitter, dreading the moment when I had to tell my team mates that I was probably leaving to join Rennes.
Hey Tito! Long time no see! Aren't you training any more?
Well then! Where have you been?
I had a trial at Rennes and guess what, guys? I got selected....
Woooooow! I knew it, you are a great footballer, Tito.
Yes you are!! Congratulations Tito! Well done!
Thanks guys! Now I have to go and tell the coach because his approval counts a lot for me.
Ok I'm going!
Good morning, coach.
Gaffer, I have never been to a training centre, I want to go.
Good morning ,Tito, how're you doing? You must know I'm not very happy with you. Rennes called me to say you were doing a trial at their club.
You are not leaving here. Now go and train with your mates.
I'll see what I can do to help you.
OK gaffer!
At the end of the season, angry as I was for not being transferred to Rennes, I had started feeling depressed, but my coach at Levallois said some nice things to cheer me up and decided to help me find a new club.

A little while later, I was contacted by Paris St Germain. I couldn't believe it – me a big supporter of Olympic Marseille. I went for medicals which showed I had a small injury. Since the club wanted me, I went back the following day with my father, but things did not go as planned.

Yes I can see ....But now we have to pray for things to go well.

Dad, take a look at the quality of the training grounds!

You're right dad and I hope with all my heart that everything works out.

Tito, for it to happen, you'll have to work hard, meet this club's high standards if they accept you.

I know that, dad..

My boy, I insisted on coming with you but unfortunately I won't be able to stay as I have something important to do. Remain confident and bring me the contract before signing it.

My dad had hardly gone when I began to look worried, not knowing what to say first.

Make yourself comfortable Mister Drogba.

Mister Drogba we are planning on giving you a car and a very good salary if you sign with us. You know P.S.G is a big club!..

That's great! I think I will sign here.

While we were discussing this, another club official came into the office and his words really shocked me.

It's true that we are interested in having you, but you must know that it is a one year contract. You will have to approve the contract. If you get injured we will drop you because here everyone is tough.

A few moments later, while the two officials were whispering to each other, I decided to leave the office quickly for I was disappointed by what he had said. To my great surprise the same evening I got a phone call for a trial at Le Mans. I couldn't believe my ears.

Le Mans football club training grounds: a well-constructed and well equipped place.

Your facilities are absolutely amazing.

Glad you like them. We are trying to give our players very good working conditions.

That's very professional....!

Come and sign for our club, young man! We can guarantee you excellent training.

The manager gave me a complete tour of the sports facilities...

To be a football giant, Mister Drogba, you'll have to develop quickly – and we'll help you get there.

I think you've convinced me to sign for you...

Perfect! But you can still think about it, Didier. Can I call you Didier?!

Their good facilities convinced me to sign for them. But I didn't know that things would be very hard at first.

Once I was settled in Le Mans, I lived opposite Kader Seydi, one of my great friends. He had given me the nickname Tupac, the name of the famous American rap star. Why? Easy - you just had to look at me. I didn't really live the life of a professional sportsman. I was a night owl: turning up in all the town's nightclubs, treated as a VIP, wearing expensive clothes and crazy about rap music.

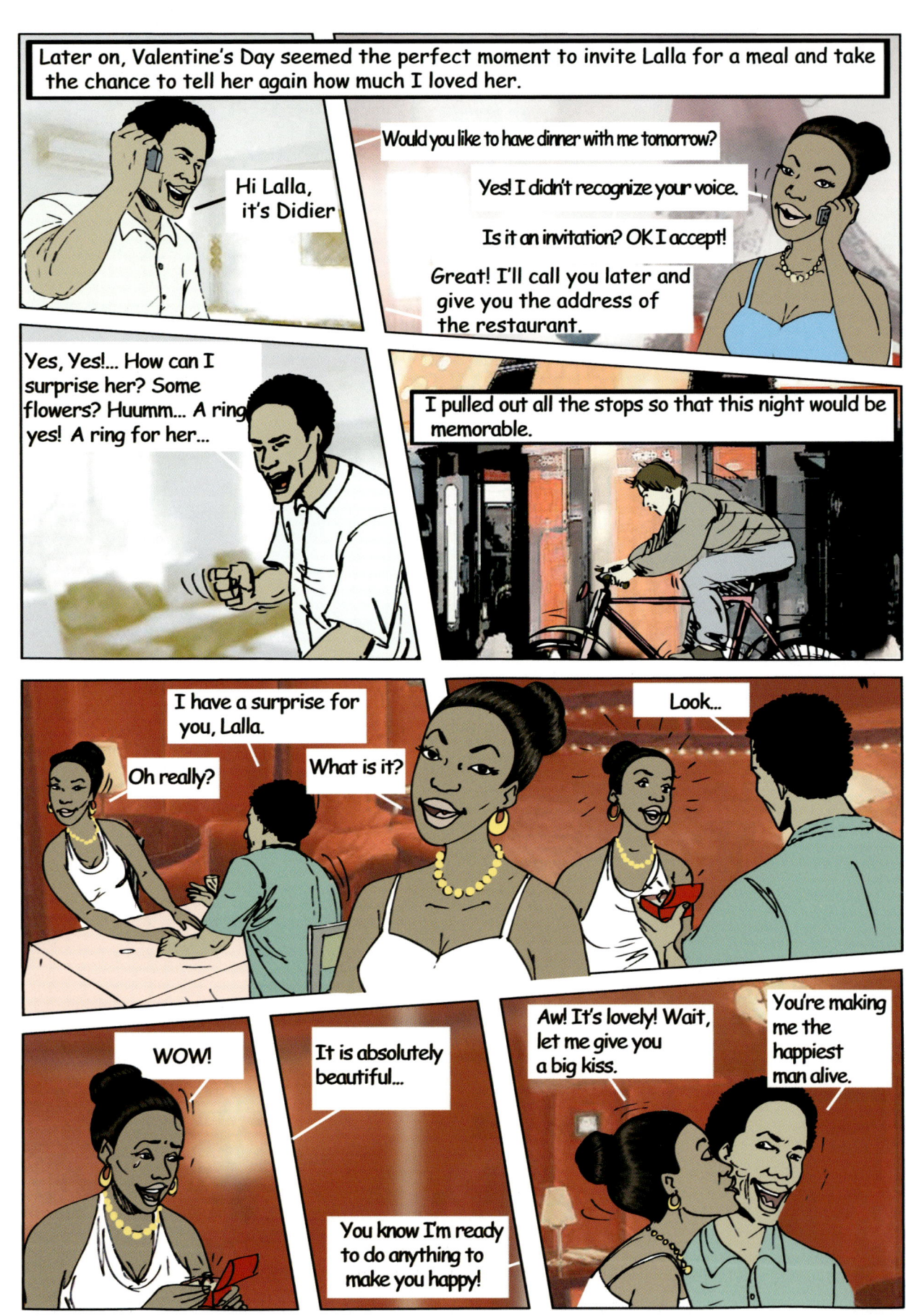

At the age of 21, I was entering the professional world through the Le Mans club. After a few matches, thanks to Thierno Seydi, who had followed me from Levallois, I signed my first professional contract with the famous football agent Pape Diouf.

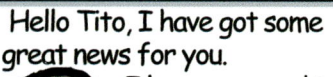

Hello Tito, I have got some great news for you.
I have managed to convince Pape Diouf to be your agent. I think this will help you a lot, man.

That's great Thierno, I can't believe it! Are you sure?...

Guys, I have to sign a contract with the famous agent Pape Diouf... it's wicked!

No, I think it's a bad idea! What are you going to do with him?

You have to manage your affairs by yourself, man.

I'm definitely going to sign for him. He's a point of reference, guys. He can make me a star.

A few hours later, I met up with Pape Diouf to talk about my contract.

Thank you for coming Mr Drogba, Thierno has told me a lot about you...

I hope he will accept me...

I believe in you and I think I can help you become a great player...

Yes that's my big ambition, Mr Diouf.

Mr Diouf, I would like to work with you so you can make me a great player. I've heard so many good things about you.

No problem, we will work together.

Thank you for your trust. Now we can talk to each other as friends. You won't regret taking me on.

From 2001 to 2003

Now that I was well settled at Le Mans, Lalla had finally decided to come often and stay with me, though she was still living at Vannes. This was during a football season which had started well for me at my club, Le Mans.

After this happy family event, my career at Le Mans continued normally until the day the trophies were awarded... A football player whom I didn't know particularly well, Reginald Ray, came up to me and I remembered a bit of our conversation: this team mate insisted that I should believe in my career and take myself in hand. His words were: "Listen Didier, with your skill as a player and your build you shouldn't let yourself be dropped from the team. For six months be serious - I know that you do mess around a lot". These few words triggered something in me and made me keen to boost my career... That's when things started moving forward with an offer from Guingamp to put me in their team. But I could not get hold of Thierno and it was difficult for me to commit myself until I had contacted Pape Diouf. His experience and confidence led me to sign the contract.

This bold decision meant I could join the Guingamp team in 2002 and had the luck to play beside an intelligent and determined player, Florent Malouda who became a close friend....

TITO!

TITO!

TITO!

GOOOOOOOOOAAAAA...

PAF

Hey!! This Didier Drogba. What a terrific player! He has just scored a superb goal! We should also mention that he got the ball from a perfect pass by his team-mate Malouda ...
And it was 1-0 to Guingamp.

In fact the positive development of my career had just started! When I was peacefully sitting at the TV with my wife, the phone rang...I had no idea that my life was going to be closely linked to the Ivorian people, but...

Hello, good morning. This is the Ivorian Football Association. May I speak to Mr Didier Drogba?

Yes it's me, speaking.

You have been invited to play for the Ivory Coast national team in a game against South Africa...

You should know that the country needs you.

Thank you! I am honoured.

Darling!..I have been invited to play for the Ivorian national team.

That's fantastic news my love! You will make your country proud!

Abidjan, the Houphouët Boigny Stadium, where I was playing my first game in the Ivory Coast national team.

From 2003 to 2004

The last season at Guingamp was a success but the desire to explore new horizons was overcoming me. It was time for me to share this with the president of the club.

Coach, I am planning on leaving the club.

Do you mean it?! Why do you want to leave? Everybody likes you here and I count on you.

I would like new adventures and new challenges....

Which club would you like to go to?

Olympic Marseille.

To OM??

The club has many plans for the next season, Didier... So try to think about it because I also intend to hang on to you...

I finally managed to make an agreement with the president of OM for your transfer. You might like to know that the president of Lyon also wanted you in his club.

I wish you good luck in this new adventure and I thank you for your efforts in our club this season.

Thank you, thank you very much, president. OM is the club of my dreams.

And thanks again for everything you have done for me.

It was 2003 and one of my dreams was about to come true...I will always remember this player, Reginald Ray, the one I met during the last award ceremony and who gave me some good advice regarding my future in football. It was thanks to him that the desire to boost my career was born in me....

Once my transfer to OM had become official, discussions were going on in La Canebière.

OM strengthens its attack capability with Didier Drogba.

Let's hope that that Didier Drogba brings a lot to OM this season!

He had a very good season at Guingamp. He's good, you'll see!

DROIT AU BUT

OM organized a press conference to introduce me officially to its public. I was wearing number 11, my lucky number.

How do you feel about defending the colours of Olympic Marseille?

It is like a dream come true for me...

What can we expect from you after joining the OM team?

The aim is to win titles and have a good season.

And for me it means scoring a lot of goals in my new team's colours.

DROGBA
11

It was specially difficult at the beginning...Our OM team had suffered a rather testing league season with the change of coach. To "go for goals" and overcome the challenge of achieving a successful season, I had to step up my efforts....

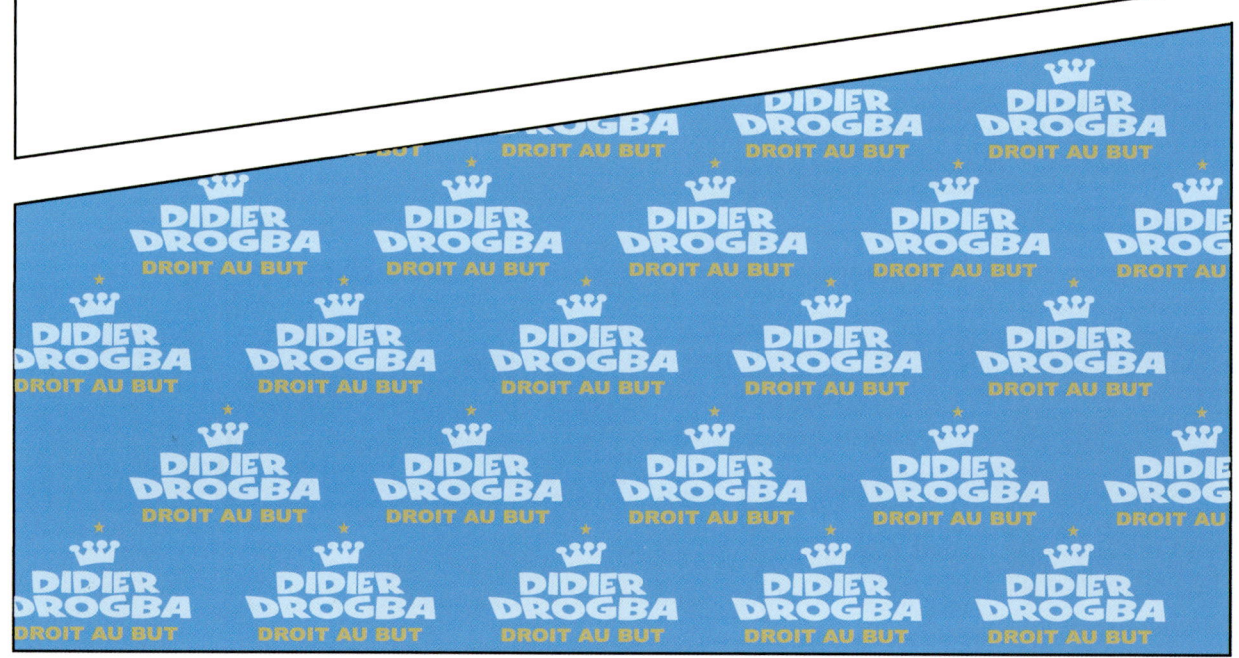

We went into all our matches with terrific enthusiasm. The atmosphere was crazy in the stadium. During the match against FC Porto, I met one of the personalities who helped me become a great player.

We are watching a beautiful game between OM and FC Porto. The Marseille crowd is very supportive this evening! It's half-time and we are also going to take a break to breathe a bit, so now back to the studios.

INTO THE GOAL!

STRAIGHT INTO THE GOAL, GUYS!

We have to please the public.

In the corridor to the changing rooms, Mourinho, the FC Porto coach, saw me and asked...

Excuse-me, have you got a minute?

Yes Sir.

Tell me, do you have a cousin or a brother like you? As I don't have enough money in FC Porto to recruit you....

Ha ha ha, I understand now but I don't think I have a brother or a cousin like me – I'm unique!.

But if you find one, let me know.. HA HA HA....

TITO

OK Hahaha...

TITO

After being sadly knocked out of the Champions' League, OM seems to be doing better in the UEFA Cup. We were getting ready to face the famous English team, Liverpool. We were highly motivated...

The same energy was coming from the OM supporters in the stadium...

During our away game at Anfield, the Liverpool stadium, the strong Liverpool team was leading 1-0 at the beginning of the second half. I was lucky enough to equalise for my team - I had promised myself to play a great game that day.

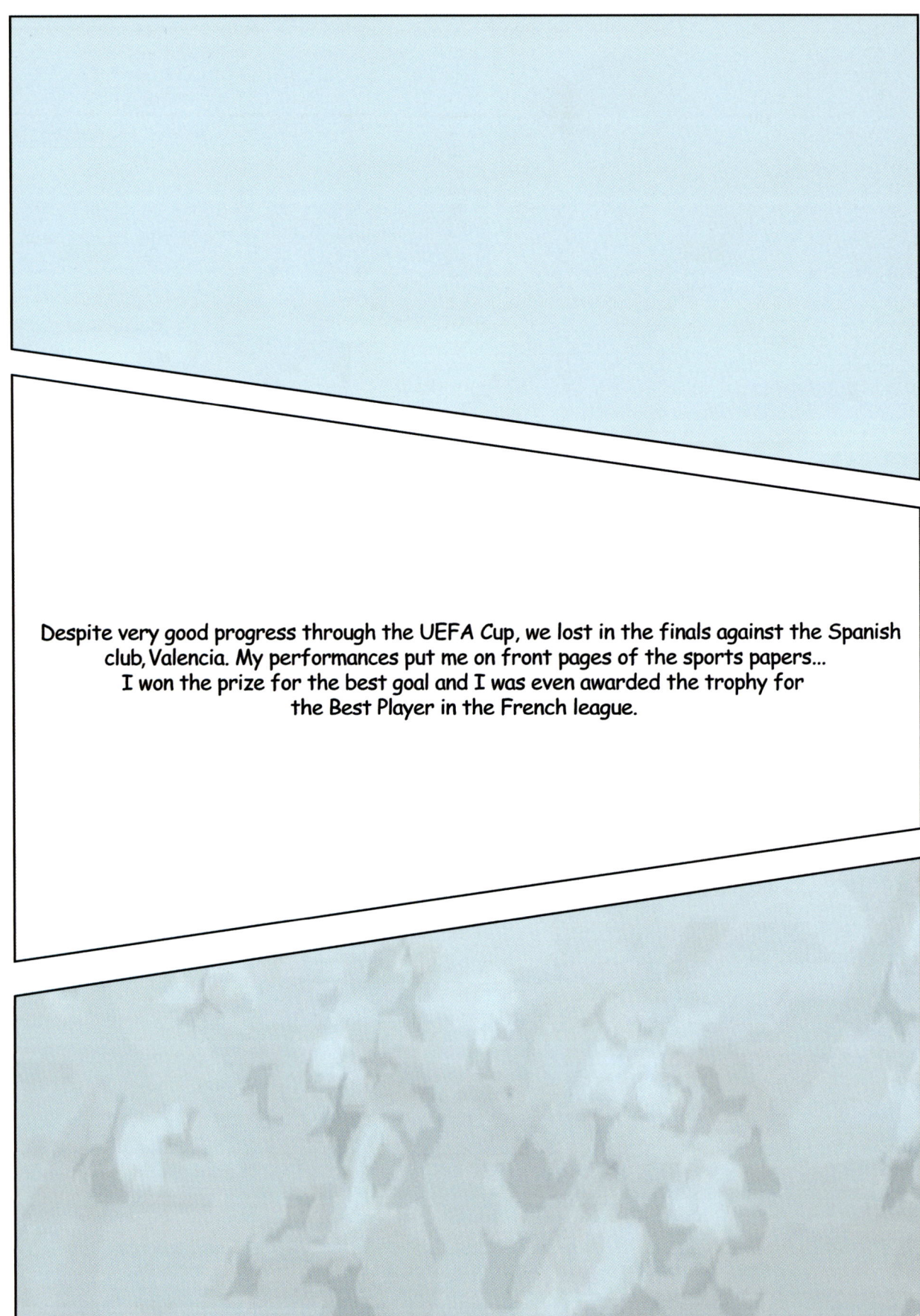

Despite very good progress through the UEFA Cup, we lost in the finals against the Spanish club, Valencia. My performances put me on front pages of the sports papers...
I won the prize for the best goal and I was even awarded the trophy for
the Best Player in the French league.

After rumours of transfers into different great clubs, I found out through a journalist that a transfer deal was almost finalised with an English club...

Drogba are you aware of what's going on? An English club has allegedly made an offer for you, I don't know the name of the club but I'll tell you if I find out...

That's not a problem. Don't worry, don't look for it. Anyway I am not moving.

Hello Thierno, it seems that an English club is trying to recruit me?

Yes but we will talk about it when you come back from Cameroon.

OK, but I don't want to leave OM!

Important negotiations were going on about my transfer, so Pape Diouf decided to come to Cameroon to convince me to go ahead with the transfer.

Hello Pape?!

Yes Thierno, how are you?

We must do everything to convince Didier to sign with Chelsea. It is a golden opportunity for his career.

OK don't worry, I am going to meet him in Cameroon!

As promised to Thierno, Pape Diouf came to visit me in Cameroon where I was on tour with the Ivorian national team.

YAOUNDE Sports Stadium. Game: Cameroon v. Ivory Coast.

Pape Diouf found me at the Mont Fébé Hotel where all the team were staying before the game against the "Indomitable Lions of Cameroon"...

We think that you should accept Chelsea's offer...It is very important for your career. OM has accepted Chelsea's offer. The club is ready to sell you.

I understand what you are saying, Pape, but I don't want to leave OM. I feel at home there.

Listen to me, Didier, if you go to Chelsea you will be able to provide for your family for ever.

But what should I do...? On one hand, I don't want to leave Marseille 'cause I really like the club... on the other hand, if Pape has come all the way out here, it must mean that this transfer is really important.

As a big brother to you, I am telling you that you can't refuse the offer. With this contract you will have the means to make sure that your family does not lack anything for the rest of your life.

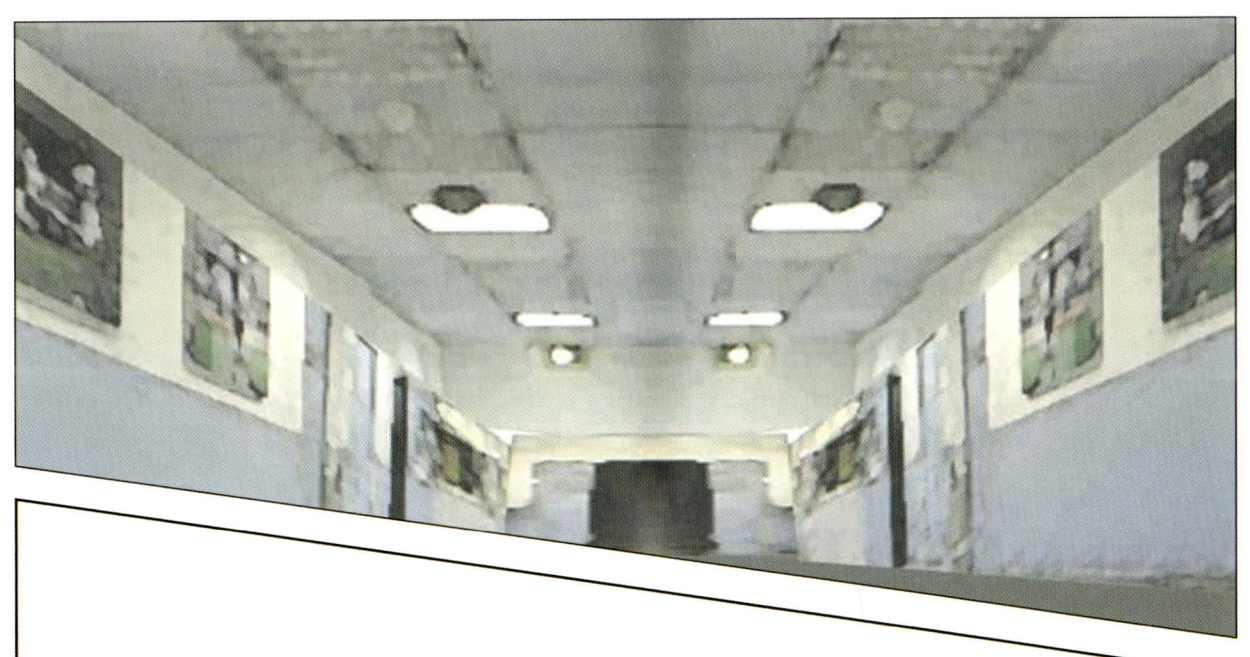

Returning to Marseille, journalists were waiting for me to announce my departure from
OM officially at a press conference... Despite the offer of big money by Chelsea,
I was very sad at the thought of leaving La Canebière... I saw my departure from
OM as a veritable act of treason of the President of the club.

56

And so begins the adventure "From Tito to Drogba…"

A new step in my life starts with the signature of this new contract with the English club, Chelsea. It is a new challenge for the pride of the Ivorian people and of the African continent.

I can already hear my supporters and fans shouting with joy at all my moves and my goals in the iconic Stamford Bridge stadium and in other great stadiums all over Europe....Follow me into new adventures in the rough world of the English championship and of the prestigious international football competitions...

I'll bring you more gripping stories full of challenges and self-sacrifice, full of joy and tears, of disappointment and victories.... I invite you to share with me some excitement, so many amazing moments which we can experience together in the next volume...

www.titodrogba.com

THANKS

Didier **DROGBA**

Thierno **SEYDI**

Etienne **MENDY**, Touti and Balil **MENDY**

Pierre **SAUVALLE** - Studio PICTOON

Mamadou **BAMBA**, Dominique **KHALIF** - Orange Côte d'Ivoire

Nicolas Omar **DIOP** aka **NIX**

Rodrigue **ZIKE**, Joël **LEKI** - 100% Free

Phillippe **JUPIN** aka **JUJU** - La Bellevilloise

François **KONIAN** - Radio Jam

Landry Watonn **IPAUD** – HB

DAWALA, BAMS – WATI B

Guillaume **BERTEL** - COMQUEST

Dieudonné **GNAMMANKOU** - DAGAN Edition

Félix **ANAGONOU** - Esprit Libre Junior

Family **GUEHI BAO**, Mathias **MILLER**, Guy-Roland **TANOH**, Nelly **PIRES**,
His Exellency Simon **TONGE** et Madame, Hamma **N'DIAYE**, Youssouf **TOURE**
Aicha **BAMBA CHONE**, Eva **ANNETTE**, Germain **DJIDA**, Marianne **NKAMTCHOUM**,
Abiba **SAKANOGO**, Nadine **DRAMA**, Michel et Thierry **KIRI**, Hippolyte **KOUAME**,
Philippe **PANZINI**, Kemi **ZINSOU**, Oumar **YERE**, Leila **THIOUB**, Marinette **NDANGUI**,
Paul-Aimée **DOSONGUI**, Magloire **DANIN**,
Christelle Natacha **BOUA**, Nora **NGUEMA**
Stéphanie **KOUADIO**, Cédric **CAPO CHICHI**, Fatim **TOURE**, Marie Patrice Watonn **IPAUD**,
Assane **SYLLA**, Thomas **MOULARE**, Vincent **KACOU**, Jessica **NANOU-WAOTA**,
Hervé **POOSSON**, Stéphanie **VIEL**, Guy-Michel **BOLI**, Josiane **NGUESSAN MORENO**,
Fabiola **MENIE**, Issa **BADIANE**.
Jöel **AMANI,** Anne Maryse **KHABORE**, Daouda **DIABATE**
Roméo **ZAGADOU**, Fatou **KABA**, Andy **COSTA**, Christian **OBROU**
Gregory **CHOPLIN**, Mamery **FADIGA**, Clarisse **ANGORAN**, George **TAPAI**,
Le Célèbre **BAUZA**, Ouraye **DIAKITE** Caroline **Mc ATEER**, **KANON** Hervé